To my mom and step dad, for watching me play.
For my dad, who watched with the angels.
To my brothers, for letting me play.
To D, for making this happen.

ACKNOWLEDGMENTS

Thanks for being my 'athletic supporters'!

Rita J. Runyon
Carmen Jones
Thom Loverro
Tami Barone
Fatima Warren
Princess Agra
Danielle Balmelle
Danielle Carr
Bev Pensick
Sandra Shaughnessy
Cristalle Shelton
Colvin Underwood
Doc Walker
Dave Weinberger

CONTENTS

INTRODUCTION

WARNING:
This book is intended for the sole purpose of stimulating a woman's mind through the game of football. Any other use is strictly forbidden! Gaining some understanding of men is purely coincidental.

Football may be a so-called man's sport, but girlfriend, it's time for you to get in the game! You see, along with football, sports like baseball, basketball, and hockey get a man's adrenaline going, but we can't forget the most important sport of all, WOMEN. Yes ladies, you too may be a sport just as men can be to women. Plus, it's not easy to find a guy who prefers to hang out with you at the mall on the weekend, so you might want to get to know something about football. Trust me, it can be for your own good. And hopefully, this book will lead to a long and lasting relationship with the game of football and who knows what else! You really can LEARN TO LOVE IT and he may just love you more for trying!

Now time is of the essence. LEARN TO LOVE IT– *A 'quickie' guide to men and pro football in 60 minutes* means you should be able to do this all in about one hour. Which, coincidentally happens to be the amount of time in a pro football game. It's played in four 15-minute quarters for a total length of 60 minutes. That should be easy for you to remember.

However, add commercial breaks, time outs, etc. and the game actually goes on for almost 3 hours. But you know how guys are! They seem to think that making it last longer, is always better!

It's also imperative that you don't skip any chapters and miss some important information. You don't want to get lost. Of course, most women would stop to ask for directions if that happened, but you can avoid getting lost by reading through from beginning to end.

Please note that there are some differences between high school, college and professional football. In this book, you'll get a quick and basic understanding of the intimate game of professional or PRO FOOTBALL. The 'intimate' part being when the guys hug, hold hands or pat each other on the rear after a great moment in the game!

Knowing something about football can also help YOU 'score' both personally and professionally in the game of life. Think about it. Knowing what your male co-workers are saying about Sunday's game during the Monday morning breakfast meeting can certainly be a benefit. Imagine how impressed they'll be when you add, "and can you believe they went for it on 4th and 1", and really know what you're talking about! While you're at it, catch the look on the face of your man when you know the team is going to pass on 3rd and long!

And what about all of the innuendos that are sports related? "Score a touchdown, Hit a home run, That's a slam dunk." It's about time you become an active player and understand what guys are talking about. You've heard their lines and you know that **"A GOOD LINE IS EVERYTHING"**.

A GOOD LINE IS EVERYTHING

There's nothing worse than a bad line. Many women have heard more than their share, and know that the good lines have a better chance to score at some point down the road. The most important thing to remember is that football is the same way. A good offensive line can help get you there. And where is there? The end zone. That's where a touchdown is scored, where points are made that hopefully win the game.

Before we plunge into that area, you need to know about some other lines, the ones that help make up the football field. Now mind you, this part is not too exciting, but you'll just have to deal with it for a moment as with other lines that you may have heard! To help you visualize all of these lines, check out this diagram of a football field.

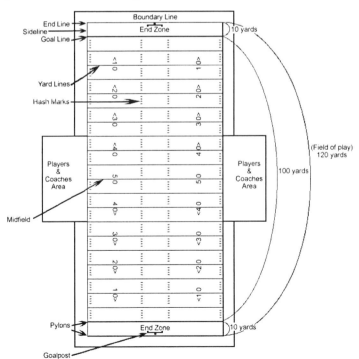

The rectangular field is 120 yards long and just over 53 yards wide. A white line several feet wide is painted around the field as a border. The players or the football are *out of bounds* if this border, known as the *boundary line*, is touched. Being *in bounds* requires staying within the boundary line in the *field of play.* You're either in or out. You know how that is. There are a couple of parts to the boundary line. Simple enough, the longer two sides are the *sidelines*. The shorter ends are the *end lines*.

The major white line on the field is the *goal line*. The goal of the game is to cross the other team's goal line the most to score more points and win the game. Ladies, this just happens to be one of those times when crossing the line is a good thing. The goal line is 10 yards from the end line. The space in between represents the *end zone.* A player crossing the goal line and entering the end zone with the ball is a climax in the game. Hopefully, this moment can be achieved more than once, a theory foreign to some guys. Even in the game of football, ultimate success is defined by repeating an outstanding performance!

There are two end zones, one at each end of the field. The four corners of the end zone are marked by a soft orange *pylon*, which is also in bounds when touched by a player or the football. A player, with the ball who touches a pylon before any part of his body touches down or out of bounds, has just scored a touchdown.

Standing at the back of the end zone is a tall erect structure called a *goalpost*. It has a *crossbar* connecting two poles called *uprights*. Kicking the ball through the uprights can also score points. How to score is just ahead.

Now in order to get to the goal line and into the end zone, a team has some other lines to cross. That would be the *yard lines*. The field has 100 yards in between the goal lines, which are split in to two sides of 50 yards each. At the middle of the field, known as *midfield,* is the 50-yard line. The yard lines are marked by number on the field in increments of 10 and stretch from sideline to sideline. Moving from the middle of the field toward each goal line is the 40, 30, 20, and 10 yard line. The 5, 15, 25, 35, and 45 yard lines also reach from sideline to sideline but the numbers are not painted on the field.

And not to leave out the rest of the yard lines, like the 1,2,3,4,6,7,8, etc. which are discreetly marked by the short lines on the field. They obviously aren't as long as the others, but what they lack in quality, they make up for in quantity. Haven't we all been there! The short yard lines are marked four times each on the field, near each sideline and in two places near the center of the field. These short lines near the center of the field are called *hash marks*, and they hold a special position. They set the guideline for where the football is placed when a play begins. The ball will always be placed somewhere in between the two center hash marks because teams need room on either side of the ball to make the play happen.

A *play* is what a team does to try to move the ball away from their end zone or home, down the field to the other team's end zone to try to score. Why are they running away from their home, you ask? To conquer another man's territory. We'll get to that later.

And just when you think you've heard all of the lines you can take, you get pummeled with a couple more. You'll have to use your imagination here. There's a line that's necessary to begin every play, but you can't see it. A play begins at this imaginary point called the *line of scrimmage*. Each team has an invisible line which stretches across the field from sideline to sideline at the point where the ball is placed on the field. The area in between those two lines where the ball is located is called the *neutral zone*. More on the neutral zone in another chapter.

And what about that yellow line on the field that appears

on your television screen. You can see it at home, but no one sees it at the game. The yellow line is a graphic television effect produced to give viewers a better idea of the point where a team needs to move the ball to get another 1st down. That part of the game is still to come.

Now that you know about lines, it's time to find out something a little more strategic. After all, everyone wants to know **"HOW TO SCORE"**.

2 HOW TO SCORE

There are several ways to score, and that's no different in football! Actually, there are only 5 ways to score in football, but at least you can learn all of these! The team trying to score will have *possession* of the ball and is called the *offense*. While one team is on offense, the other team will be on *defense*, or the defensive team.

The offense wants to move the ball forward towards the opponent's end zone while the defense tries to prevent the offensive team's advances. Scoring can happen on the ground or in the air and here's how it goes. The football can be carried by a player or passed from one to another into the opposing team's end zone to score a *touchdown*, also known as a *TD*. If the offense is successful in penetrating the opponent's end zone, the team earns 6 points for a touchdown. Six definitely sounds a little like a score, doesn't it? After the touchdown, a team has a couple of options to add some extra points, which is always a good idea.

Kicking the ball through the uprights is worth one point and is called a *P-A-T*, a *point-after-touchdown*, also referred to as an *extra point*. Or, a team can try to double that by running or passing the ball again to the end zone for 2 points, called a *2-point conversion*.

Sometimes a team may not be able to get into the end zone to score a touchdown. If they can't get it in, there is still hope to score! Another option involves kicking the ball through the uprights of the goalpost to get 3 points, which is called a *field goal*. Those are the ways the offense can score some points, but the defense sometimes knows a thing or two about scoring.

Yes, turn about is fair play. The defense can earn 2 points for their team with something called a *safety*. They can also take the ball away from the offense and score a touchdown. That's a little bit more technical and will be explained later on.

Again, the 5 ways to score in football are:

Touchdown - 6 points

Point-after-touchdown - 1 point

2-point conversion - 2 points

Field Goal - 3 points

Safety - 2 points

Now that you know how to score, don't you think it's time you learned **"HOW TO BE A PLAYER"**?

3 HOW TO BE A PLAYER

Getting lucky could have been on some man's mind when determining the number of players on the field at one time. Seven and eleven are considered to be lucky numbers and coincidentally or not, those numbers are a part of football.

Each team must have 11 players on the field for every play that happens in a game. No more, no less. But believe it or not, there is such a thing as too many men in the game of football. If a team has more than eleven players on the field during a play, they will get penalized. More on the 'penalized' word later on in the book.

As for the eleven players on the field, the defense can position their guys in any different way they choose behind their line of scrimmage (that imaginary line). The offense, however, must always have at least seven players up front on their line of scrimmage when a play begins. They make up the *offensive line*. The remaining offensive players are behind that offensive line and are called the *backfield*.

The backfield includes the most important offensive player on the team, the *quarterback*. Sometimes referred to as the *Q-B*, the quarterback runs the show and can hand the ball off to a player behind him called a *running back* (a guy who runs the ball). The majority of the time you will see two running backs in the game. However, depending on the play, you may see one running back or several on the field at once.

If the Q-B doesn't hand off the ball, he will throw the ball to a player called a *receiver*. If a receiver catches the ball in bounds, it is a *complete pass* or *pass completion*. If the pass is not caught or is caught out of bounds, it is an *incomplete pass* or *incompletion*. Sometimes, a running back will also get a chance to catch the ball like a receiver and occasionally a receiver may also run the ball.

15

Nevertheless, anyone who runs with the ball is said to be the *ball carrier*. There are times when the Q-B will even run the ball himself, but that usually happens only when he has no other choice.

That brings us to that all-important offensive line that was mentioned at the beginning of this book. If the *offensive linemen* are doing their job right, the quarterback won't have to run for his life. When the defense breaks through the offensive line and threatens to *tackle* or *sack* the quarterback while he is behind the line of scrimmage, the Q-B tries to avoid the defense by running away or *scrambling*, like a man trying to avoid commitment!

It is the offensive line's duty to protect the quarterback and keep the defense from getting to him or any other player who has the ball. That's why the offensive line is so important and a good one is very valuable. The key guy on the offensive line is the *center*, because he's at the center of the line. The center is the only player touching the ball before a play begins. When the quarterback is giving a verbal signal called a *snap count*, the center will *snap* the ball from the ground into the hands of the quarterback. Usually, the quarterback's hands are right underneath the center's backside, or butt if you prefer, but sometimes the quarterback stands a few feet in back of the center. When the quarterback is in that position, he is said to be in the *shotgun*, meaning the center has to shoot the ball between his legs in to the air to get it to the quarterback.

Next to the center on each side of him are the *guards*. A *right guard* on the right side, and a *left guard* on his left side. The guards help the center protect the quarterback so he can successfully complete a play. They use their bodies for *blocking* the defense to keep them away from the quarterback. The center and guards may also block the defense to create an opening in the line for a player to run the ball past the defense. The center and guards get some help from the *offensive tackles*. The tackles are next to the guards on the offensive line. A *right tackle* on the right side of the right guard and a *left tackle* on the left side of the left guard. Offensive tackles aren't actually allowed to tackle anyone, but are there to help block and protect the player who has the ball. Beware of the guy who pretends to be something he's not!

A center, two guards, and two tackles makes for only five of the seven required players on the offensive line. Filling out the remaining two required positions on the line will be done by *tight ends* and *wide receivers*. A tight end is also a receiver, but he lines up tight, right next to one of the tackles at the end of the offensive line. Be sure to remember this, tight ends aren't the only football players with tight ends. Which brings us to the wide receiver who is positioned wider out on the line of scrimmage and may sometimes be referred to as a *wide out*. Most teams usually have one tight end and one wide receiver on the line of scrimmage, but there can be two tight ends in the game or more wide receivers. Receivers and running backs are interchangeable to total eleven players.

Moving on to the defense. These guys have more freedom when lining up in position to start a play. Most teams will have four players on the *defensive line*. The two guys in the middle are *defensive tackles*, a right one and a left one. On each end of the defensive line next to the tackles are amazingly enough, *defensive ends*. Yes, a right one, and a left one. These *defensive linemen* try to stop the ball carrier, or, if they think the quarterback is going to throw the ball, they may try to rush past the offensive line to sack the quarterback.

There are three more players who are positioned just behind the defensive line. These players are called *linebackers* because they back the line. Linebackers try to stop a ball carrier who makes it past the defensive line.

They also watch out for receivers in their area.

The remaining four defensive players are *defensive backs* and make up what is called the *secondary* or the *defensive backfield*. There are two players called *safeties* and two *cornerbacks*. A safety is a safe back up for the defensive line and linebackers in case a runner gets past them with the ball. A safety will also try to prevent a receiver from catching a ball in his area. The cornerbacks, also called *corners*, play, where else? In the corners of the defensive backfield. Corners watch out for receivers, but will try to stop a ball carrier if needed.

Here is a diagram of a basic offensive and defensive *formation*. In other words, how the players are positioned on the field before a play begins.

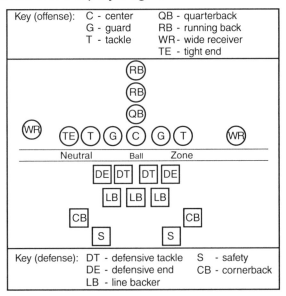

There are several different kinds of formations that teams use in a football game, but the previous diagram is one of the most basic for offense and defense. At least now you know that it takes eleven players on each team to play football, but is it possible that **"TWO CAN PLAY THIS GAME"**?

4 TWO CAN PLAY THIS GAME?

Knowing what the player positions are is important, but here's something that is even more important. If you think that guys not only get their kicks out of football, and then get the added bonus of scantily clad cheerleaders, you need to take a closer look at who can really get a good show when watching football. That would be you!

Ladies, this is a game where real men with some nice physiques are wearing very tight pants. Remember the tight end comment?

And speaking of bodies, it's pretty easy to determine a player's position based on his body type. Receivers and defensive backs tend to be the lean muscular types while the running backs and linebackers are a bit more beefy in the muscle department. Linemen are the 'lots to love' kind of guys with many weighing close to or over 300 pounds. And then you have the 'pretty boy', which usually describes the quarterback.

For those of you who prefer a little older handsome and intelligent type, you may want to look on the sidelines. That's where the coaches are. The brains behind the brawn. Each team has a *head coach* who is the top boss. The head coach usually has an *offensive coordinator* who instructs the offense and a *defensive coordinator* who instructs the defense. Or sometimes, the head coach may also hold one of those two positions as well. During a game, the plays called will come from any of these three coaches.

Rounding out the coaching staff are *assistant coaches* who specialize in specific positions such as a *running backs coach* or *defensive line coach*. These guys all have their own specific talents that they bring to the game of football. Sometimes, being a 'jack of all trades and master of none' doesn't get the job done and you have to call on an expert!

Communication between the coaches and players is

vital for the game of football. Just imagine, a group of men effectively communicating to perform a complex function time after time based on thought, skill, and timing. All they need are headsets! Coaches on the sideline wear *headsets* to talk to other coaches observing the game in a booth above the field. Even the quarterback has an earpiece attached inside of his helmet to hear the plays called. Amazing, isn't it? Who knew? The key to communicating with men is as simple as a headset. And what about that telephone on the sideline? Expecting a call from mom? Maybe, but it's usually a 'hotline' to someone like the team's owner.

Now remember, you 'too' can play this game, as a spectator. There is definitely something for everyone! Just pick a certain player or team based on the 'qualities' that you admire and you could find yourself saying this, about watching football. **"ISN'T THAT SPECIAL"**.

 ISN'T THAT SPECIAL

One motivating factor behind learning something about football is being able to spend some 'special' time with your guy, or guys, whatever your case may be. And 'special' is something you will want to remember about the game itself. Along with offensive and defensive players, some guys get the chance to be 'special' as well. These guys make up the *special teams*. Special teams come into the game, appropriately, at special times including during the kickoff, punting the ball, going for a field goal, trying for an extra point after a touchdown or attempting the 2-point conversion if they want to try for two points.

Because a team can only have 45 players listed on their *roster* during a game, some of the offensive and defensive players may also get assigned to special team duty. Being versatile is definitely an advantage when it comes to playing football. Some players could even be in on all of the special teams while still having to play either offense or defense. Usually those are the younger players, because they have more stamina! Could that explain why some older women date younger men?

Special teams are also special because they are on the field first to start the game. The beginning of a football game always begins with a *kickoff*. The player who is the *kicker* will set the football on a *tee*. When the signal is given, the kicker will run to the ball and kick it off to the other team. That team will then try to have a player catch the ball and run it back as far as he can. The player who catches the kicked ball is called the *kick returner* because he is trying to return the ball back to the other end zone. Returning something a man has just given you may not make much sense to women, but that is what happens in the game of football.

Sometimes the kick returner will run all the way back to

the opponent's end zone to score a touchdown. But more often, the kick returner gets tackled to the ground and his offensive teammates then come on to the field to take over at that point. The team that just kicked off will then have their defense take the field as well.

When the offense is not capable of scoring a touchdown, they will have two options. They will either have to *punt* the football to the other team, or if they are close enough, they may try for a field goal. The group of 11 players attempting a field goal is called the *field goal unit*. They will have their kicker attempt to boot the ball through the uprights of the goalpost. If the team has to punt the ball away, they bring in a different kind of kicker, called a *punter*. His job and title are different because a teammate will snap the ball to him, he'll have to catch it and drop kick it or punt it to the other team. And remember, it's never a good thing when your team has to 'punt'. After all, **"FOOTBALL REALLY IS A LIFE OR DEATH SITUATION"**.

FOOTBALL REALLY IS A LIFE OR DEATH SITUATION

Sometimes one would think that a football game was actually a life or death situation based on the reaction of certain individuals. The truth is, there is some truth to that. In the game of football, the ball itself is always one of two things, 'live or dead'.

A play begins with the snap and as soon as the center moves the ball to snap it to the quarterback, the ball is said to be *live*. When the play is over, the ball is *dead*. A play is ruled dead when an *official* blows the whistle to signal the end of the play. The 'live and dead' status of the ball continues for each play until the end of the game. During a kickoff, the ball is considered live as soon as it is kicked off the tee.

The 'live and dead' ball thing also comes in to play when players do something wrong. When a player does something 'dirty' to another player, or doesn't follow the rules, he and his team get punished. Don't get too excited, the chapter on 'punishment' is still ahead. But there's something else to arouse your interest. It's **"TIME TO GET DOWN AND DIRTY"**.

7 TIME TO GET DOWN AND DIRTY

Getting down and dirty can be a good thing. Football certainly can be a dirty game. No explanation needed here. The 'down' part is a little more complicated but extremely important.

After a team receives the ball on a kickoff or punt, their offense will next take the field and get four plays to move the ball forward a distance of at least 10 yards. The forward movement of the football is called *forward progress*. The offense must gain at least 10 yards in those four plays in order to keep possession of the ball.

Before that first play begins, the ball is 'down' on the field. The offense will then attempt the first play or *down* to move the ball 10 yards. The term '1st down and 10 yards to go' is used to describe the situation. It may also be referred to as '1st and 10'. After that 1st down play, the ball is again 'down' on the field for the offense to attempt their 2nd down. Depending on how many yards the offense gained, or possibly lost on the 1st down, determines the yards to go for the 2nd down.

Imagine that the offense moved the ball forward and gained 6 yards on the 1st down play. The offense made 6 of the necessary 10 yards, which means they need 4 more yards to equal 10. They are now in a '2nd down and 4 yards to go' situation to get those 10 yards. On the 2nd down play, suppose the offense gains another 3 yards. The offense gained 6 yards on the 1st down plus 3 yards on the 2nd down, for a total of 9 yards in two downs. On the next play, the offense is said to be in a '3rd down and 1 yard to go' situation.

Let's say the offense moved the ball 1 yard on the 3rd down to gain that total of 10 yards. When that happens, the offense has earned another *set of downs* and will continue to play with 4 more chances and another '1st down and 10 yards to go' situation. It's probably no coincidence that football is a game where men are trying for as many chances to score as possible. But what if, on the 3rd down, the offense didn't gain that 1 yard to total 10 yards?

Remember there are 4 downs to make those 10 yards, so they still would have a 4th down opportunity. That's where the options come in. A team has three options on a 4th down situation. They can punt the ball, try for a field goal, or take a risk and simply go for it. To quote, 'go for it' on 4th down and 1 means the offense absolutely must make that final yard. If they don't, the other team will gain possession of the ball and have their offense take over on the field at the point where the other team left it. Sometimes another chance pays off, sometimes it doesn't. We certainly know how that goes, don't we ladies? To help you understand this in football terms, you've got to remember, **"IT'S A TERRITORIAL THING"**.

8 IT'S A TERRITORIAL THING

Since the beginning of civilization, men have been associated with this 'territorial thing'. Many wars have been and will continue to be fought over territory and that can include women. You can prevent one of these conflicts by not dating a friend of your ex! In the game of football, each team also has its' own territory to defend and you can bet that any territory gained will be properly marked.

As mentioned earlier, each team has their own end zone in football and must defend it by preventing the other team from crossing the goal line in to their end zone. Each team's end zone is referred to as their 'own end zone' and their goal line is referred to as their 'own goal line'. The half of the field from each teams 'own end zone' up to the 50-yard line is referred to as each team's 'own end', or *territory*. Let's break it down. The field is 120 yards in length. It's split in half with each team's territory consisting of 50 yards of playing field and 10 yards of end zone totaling 60 yards. Those last 10 yards of end zone are the most sacred to protect.

The yard lines in each team's territory are referred to as their 'own yard line'. For example, when a team is on their 'own 20-yard line', they are 80 yards from the opposing team's end zone. Now to keep things interesting and fair, teams switch territory and end zones at the end of each of the four quarters. That's done because of the effects of Mother Nature and human nature. More specifically, unruly weather and annoying fans.

Marking the position of the ball and its progress are crucial in the game of football. The marking process is kept in check on the sideline. It's important to know the spot of the ball (what yard line it's on), the down, and how far a team needs to go to earn another 1st down, which is also called the *necessary line*. The line necessary for a 1st down is also that yellow graphic line you see on television. On the sideline, a ten-yard long chain keeps track of the necessary line for a 1st down with two very tall markers on each end. The guys who hold up the markers during the game are the *chain gang*. Easy now, they are not allowed to take the chains home! There is a third member of the group who holds the *down marker.* That marker displays the number of the down at the point where the ball is spotted. In the event of a close call the officials will bring the chains out on the field to measure for a 1st down.

Now in order to put this territory thing into perspective, it's time to rev up the engine in **"GOING FOR A LITTLE DRIVE"**.

9 GOING FOR A LITTLE DRIVE

They say the best way to really get to know a man is to take a drive together. Where else can you get several hours of his undivided attention? Then again, understanding a drive in football could help too. A *drive* is what you call the series of plays a team runs while they are on offense. So let's take an imaginary drive and see how it goes.

Before we go on this drive, we have to set the stage. The game is about to begin between the Red team and the Blue team. Before the teams take the field, there is a *coin toss* to determine who will kick off and who will receive the ball. It's sort of like deciding who gets to drive first. The winner of the coin toss has their choice and will elect to kick off or receive. The team that will kick off to start the 1st half will later receive the ball to start the 2nd half.

The Blue team won the toss and elected to receive the ball. On the opening kick off, the Red's special team unit has kicked off to the Blue's special team unit. The Blue team will try to drive the ball down the field first. The Blue team's kick returner catches the ball in his own end zone and returns it for 20 yards as he is tackled at the 20-yard line in his team's own territory. The Blue team's offense then takes the field to begin their first set of downs. During the game, you will hear the announcer say something like this before the Blue team's offense runs their first play — "The Blue team opens up with a 1st down and 10 at their own 20-yard line".

But before we get to the 1st play of the game, there is some important business to take care of. In fact, before every play in the game, a little foreplay takes place. It's that tender moment between players called a *huddle*. The players on the field are huddled together and often hold hands while the Q-B tells the offense what play will be run and on what word of the snap count the center will snap the ball. On defense, one of the linebackers informs the players as to what play has been called for them.

There seems to be a lot of hand holding going on here as well. Notice the players on the sideline at the end of a close game. They're holding hands, too. If your man won't hold your hand in public, maybe you should join a football team! Back to the 1st down play. The Blue team calls a running play. The ball is snapped by the center to the quarterback who hands the ball off to a running back. He gains 6 yards up to their own 26-yard line. That brings up the Blue team's 2nd down and because they gained 6 yards, they now have 4 yards to go to equal the 10 yards needed for another 1st down. The announcer then says "2nd down and 4 from the Blue team's own 26-yard line".

Because the Blue team is in their own territory and not very far from their own end zone, they'll likely run the ball again on a 2nd and 4 situation. The reasoning behind this play call is that they are only 26 yards from their 'own end zone'. Passing the ball is sometimes too risky this early in the game. The pass could be caught or intercepted by the Red team's defense. That would put the Red team very close to their opponent's end zone and in good position to score.

As expected, the Blue team runs the ball again on the 2nd down. They gain 5 yards this time moving the ball up to their own 31-yard line. Gaining a total of 11 yards in 2 plays, the Blue team has earned another 1st down. The ball is 'marked' or spotted at the 31-yard line and the next set of 4 downs begins with a '1st down and 10 at the Blue team's own 31-yard line'.

The Blue team appears to be having some success running the ball against the Red team so the Blue team's coach decides to continue running the ball. On '1st down and 10 at their own 31', the Blue team gets great blocking from their offensive linemen. This opens up a hole in the line for the running back to run straight up the middle of the field for a gain of 18 yards as he is tackled down at the Blue team's own 49-yard line. 18 yards on that 1st down play is a big gain and has earned the Blue team another 1st down situation. Doing the same thing over again and even better the next time definitely has its rewards!

But as you know, some good things don't last long. Or does it really have to be long to be good? Anyway, on '1st and 10 from their own 49-yard line', the Blue team is just 1 yard from midfield. Running the ball has been working so far for the Blue team, so they run it again. But this time, the Red team stops the run and tackles the running back before he is able to gain any yards. Since there is no gain, that brings up a '2nd down and still 10 yards to go from the Blue team's own 49-yard line'.

The last play may not have worked as the Blue team got 'stuffed' trying to run the ball on that 1st down. However, the coach continues to go with what he knows and plays it safe by running the ball again. Could this be an example of a man scared to take a risk? On '2nd and 10 from their own 49-yard line' the Blue team's running back runs the ball past the 50-yard line and into the Red team's territory. He is tackled at the Red team's 45-yard line for a 6 yard gain.

Here is how you calculate that 6 yard gain. Remember that once a team gets past the 50-yard line into the other team's territory, the numbers on the yard lines begin to decrease. From the Blue team's own 49-yard line to the 50 or midfield is 1 yard. Then declining yardage past midfield to the 45 is another 5 yards for a total gain of 6 yards on that 2nd down play. That brings up a '3rd down and 4 for the Blue team at the Red team's own 45-yard line'.

On 3rd and 4, the Blue team runs the ball again and gains 8 yards to the Red team's own 37-yard line which is good enough for another 1st down. The Blue team is in good field position and getting close to scoring a field goal or touchdown. That's a serious situation for the Red team as they try to slow down the Blue team by **"SLAMMING ON THE BRAKES"**.

10 SLAMMING ON THE BRAKES

Slamming on the brakes is a good way to end someone's drive or stop a score! Ladies should be very familiar with that defensive move. Hey, it happens! The Blue team has a '1st and 10 from the Red team's 37-yard line' and tries to pass the ball this time. The Red team's defense breaks through the offensive line and sacks the quarterback in the backfield at the Red team's 40-yard line. That pushes the Blue team back for a moment with a loss on the play. Minus 3 yards brings up a 2nd down situation and now 13 yards to get another 1st down. And just so you know, the quarterback is the only player who can ever be sacked. Any other player brought down behind the line of scrimmage has been tackled. Announcing that a running back has just been sacked would be a huge mistake and could get you ejected from the game!

While the Red team's defenses were up for a minute, just that quickly the Blue team's offense got back in the groove of things. On '2nd down and 13 for the Blue team from the Red team's own 40-yard line', the quarterback passes to a receiver. He catches the ball at the 20-yard line and then runs it 20 more yards in to the Red team's end zone for a touchdown. The receiver goes crazy, does some original dance moves and throws the ball down on the field, also known as *spiking the ball*. You have just witnessed football ecstasy! And somewhere under the cheers you will hear the announcer say "the Blue team scores on a 40-yard touchdown pass". The Blue team earns six points for the TD and tries for the point after the touchdown.

Special teams take the field for the extra point attempt. The kick by the place kicker goes through the uprights and is good for one point. The Blue team leads the Red team 7-0. Once a team has scored, it is then their turn to kick off to the other team.

The team with the most points at the end of the four quarters wins the game. If neither team has an advantage, the score is tied and goes in to *overtime* or *O-T* where the first team to score any points is victorious.

A lot of territory was covered in the last few chapters, but there is another piece of real estate that should be recognized. The neutral zone mentioned earlier in this book is the ground in between the two teams' lines of scrimmage where the football is positioned on each play. The only player who can be in that territory before a play begins is the center who has his hand on the ball in order to snap it to the quarterback. Any other player in the neutral zone territory is not supposed to be there. Try telling a man that a certain spot is off limits and see what happens **"WHEN YOU DON'T FOLLOW THE RULES"**.

11 WHEN YOU DON'T FOLLOW THE RULES

Trying to get away with something in the game of football isn't quite as easy as in real life. Imagine having seven men constantly around your guy to make sure he's following the rules. That's how many officials it takes to see that the players and coaches are following all of the rules in a football game.

The officials enforcing the rules wear the black and white stripes. Isn't that ironic! The seven officials each have special areas to watch in a game. They throw a weighted gold *penalty flag* on the field when they see that a player has committed a crime.

After the penalty flag is thrown and an official has used his whistle to signal the end of a play, the men in stripes gather to consult each other about the rule violation and determine what violation or *foul* actually occurred. Then the head official, also called the *referee*, indicates the ruling by using hand signals and announces the crime and punishment to be handed down. You will always be able to spot the referee from the other officials. The referee wears a white cap, while the other six officials sport black ones.

Now the punishment isn't as easy as black and white. Each faux pas or foul has it's own specific *penalty* assessed. I think you know how that works! A penalty, however, has one main objective to move the team who fouled up further away from their opponent's goal line.

If the offense messes up, the football would be moved backwards and yards are taken away from them. If the defense goofs up, they are penalized by moving the ball back towards them so that the offense gains some yards. How's that for a lesson in give and take?

A team may also decide to decline a penalty assessed to their opponent. In some cases, accepting the penalty may not be to a teams' advantage.

Penalizing the guys is never an easy task. Some errors in judgment are definitely more serious than others and that's why you **"LET THE PUNISHMENT FIT THE CRIME"**.

12 LET THE PUNISHMENT FIT THE CRIME

Penalties can occur at anytime in a game whether the ball is live or dead. *Dead ball fouls* include *delay of game*, *false start*, *offside* and *encroachment*. Delay of game and false start are always penalties on the offense. Delay of game happens when the offense doesn't snap the ball before the *play clock* expires. A 40 second play clock is positioned above each end zone and is the amount of time teams have in between plays. The penalty for delay of game is 5 yards from the line of scrimmage. For instance, if the offense has a '1st and 10 from their own 45-yard line', the ball would be moved back to their own 40-yard line for a 5-yard penalty. That would make for a 1st down and 15-yard situation from their own 40-yard line.

A false start happens when an offensive player on the line moves from a set position before the ball is snapped. That too, is a 5-yard penalty assessed from the line of scrimmage and the down is repeated.

Offside and encroachment are violations that happen in the neutral zone. Both can be a foul on either offense or defense. When any player except for the center has any part of his body over the line of scrimmage before the ball is snapped, he is offside. A 5-yard penalty is assessed and the down is repeated. Encroachment is when any player, except for the center moves in to the neutral zone and makes physical contact with an opponent before the snap. That is also a 5-yard penalty from the line of scrimmage. Those are just four of the basic dead ball fouls.

There are also many fouls that occur during a live ball or play. Some of the most common are *facemask*, *holding*, *pass interference* and *clipping*. When a player on offense or defense accidentally grabs the protective bars or facemask of an opposing player's helmet, a 5-yard penalty is assessed. An intentional grab gets a 15-yard penalty.

And there is no holding in football either. Using hands or arms to illegally grab or hold an opponent's body or uniform is a 10-yard penalty for an offensive foul and a 5-yard penalty for a defensive foul. It may be a lesser yardage penalty on defensive holding, but the offense gets a big advantage by also being awarded an *automatic 1st down.*

Pass interference can also be an offensive or defensive penalty. Defensive players cannot make illegal contact with a receiver to prevent him from catching the ball until after he has touched the ball. If charged with this foul, the football is moved to the spot of the incident and the offense earns an automatic 1st down. This can be a huge benefit for the offense. On occasion, a receiver can also be charged with offensive pass interference for illegal contact with a defender.

Clipping is an offensive or defensive penalty as well. Everyone hates it when they hear this penalty against their team. Clipping is the illegal blocking of a player below the waist from the back. It costs the perpetrator 15 yards and an automatic 1st down if against the defense.

Now you know something about what happens to boys when they are bad, so let's move on to the good part. **"GOT TO HAVE A GOOD GAME PLAN"**.

13 GOT TO HAVE A GOOD GAME PLAN

Going in to it, you have to decide. How will you play this one? Will you be conservative, will you take risks, or will you just do what you always do? A good game plan is necessary!

Once one game is over, it's time to think about the next one. Usually the day after the game, coaches and players look at the game film. They determine what went right for them in that game and what they need to fix for the next one. That's called breaking down game film. Fortunately or unfortunately, you don't have complete videotapes of past relationships that you have to break down.

Preparation for the upcoming game begins immediately for the coaches as they look at game films of the next opponent to determine a game plan. Games are usually played on Sunday, but some games are scheduled on other days as well. If a team plays on Sunday and their next game is on Thursday, they have a shorter time to prepare than they would for another Sunday game. Playing games with less than a week in between is called a *short week*. Uh oh, short is not good.

To prepare for a game, a coach looks at the different types of offensive and defensive plays that they will encounter and how they have to approach their next game. That can be a very complicated process but there are some game strategies that are fairly consistent. Coaches will choose certain plays for different situations and then there are times when it's good to **"GO WITH WHAT YOU KNOW"**.

14 GO WITH WHAT YOU KNOW

Ever ask why men do a certain thing over and over again? Sometimes it's just safer to go with what you know. Football players have to know a lot, believe it or not. Each player has a huge amount of plays to learn that are compiled in a *playbook*. It is amazing what men can remember when they want to. The most important book to some men is the Play Book better known as the infamous Black Book.

Coaches select the plays they want to run based on these factors - the down, yards to go for a 1st down, field position, the score of the game, and the amount of time left to play.

Early in the game, when neither team has scored or the score between the teams is close, coaches will usually select offensive plays that they do best. Always good to go with what you know. On 1st or 2nd down, a team will usually run the ball if they have good blockers or running backs. They usually will throw the ball if they have good receivers and a quarterback who is an accurate passer. Running the ball is considered more conservative with an average gain of about 3 or 4 yards. Passing the ball is riskier but the yardage gains are often times much bigger averaging at least 10 yards.

Passing is riskier because of several factors. The quarterback may be rushed to throw the ball or the defenders could be closely covering the receivers thereby risking the ball being caught by the defense. If the quarterback is threatened by the defense while in the *pocket* (the area where he is protected by the blocking of his teammates), and there are no receivers open, he may have to get rid of the ball. He does that by throwing it out of bounds near a receiver so that no one can catch it and he avoids being sacked. Since when did a man making a pass become so difficult?

The quarterback may be able to avoid all of the chaos way before it happens. Before the ball is snapped, the quarterback reads the defense. That means he's actually looking at how the defense is set up and how their offensive play will work against that defense. If the Q-B sees a problem, he can change the play on the spot. He will *audible* or yell out a new play to his teammates that he thinks will work.

A couple of other clues may help you know when a team is going to run or pass the ball. When the offense needs less than 4 yards to get a first down, you can usually expect the team to run the ball. 4 yards or less is considered a 'short yardage situation'.

On a 3rd down situation with more than 5 yards to go for a 1st down, a team will usually pass the ball because they need a larger gain. 3rd and 5 or more yards is called a '3rd and long situation'. If, on the 3rd down, a team gets enough yards for a 1st down, they have successfully completed a '3rd down conversion'. And if they are unsuccessful on the 3rd down conversion, there is still the 4th down to come. So, **"WHY NOT GO FOR IT"**?

15 WHY NOT GO FOR IT?

There are times when you should and times when you should NOT go for it. It's pretty easy to tell the difference, isn't it? In football, a team has three options on the 4th down, including punting, trying for a field goal or *going for it*. Let's start with the punt. A team will usually punt the ball if they are in their own territory unless they are behind late in the game and need to score. In that case, a team has to go for it on a 4th down in order to have any chance of winning. Going for it on 4th down is obviously the team's last attempt for a 1st down. If they don't make it, the other team gets possession of the ball. Sometimes a team may go for it on a '4th and short situation' if they believe they can make it. That's not a big risk if they are ahead and in the opponent's territory. Most often, within the opponent's 30-yard line or less, a team will do the safe thing and try for a field goal instead because most field goal kickers have high percentages of making it.

There are other strategies in the kicking part of the game. If a ball is kicked into the end zone and the kick returner or punt returner thinks he doesn't have a good chance at running very far out of the end zone, he may catch the ball and take a knee. 'Taking a knee' is when a player kneels down on one knee in his own end zone which downs the ball and ends the play. The ball is then spotted for the offense at their own 20-yard line. If the ball goes past the end line on a kick off, the ball is also spotted at the 20-yard line. Both situations are called a *touchback*. A player such as the quarterback, may also intentionally 'take a knee' to down the ball during any play in the game.

When the ball is kicked or punted, but doesn't reach the end zone, the returner will try to run it back or he has a few options. He can let the ball bounce and roll on the ground until it comes to a stop, or he can call a *fair catch*.

On a fair catch, the returner raises one arm in the air during the kick or punt to signal that he will 'fair catch' the ball and not try to run with it. After the signal, the defense cannot touch him and the ball is marked down at the point of the catch.

Another strategy in football has to do with time. Each time a team has the ball, their total *time of possession* is recorded. A team that runs the ball more will usually have a longer time of possessing the ball because it takes longer to run with the ball. A passing team takes up less time because a pass is thrown very quickly. If a team is leading late in the game, they will usually run the ball to run time off the clock so the other team has less time to score. Deliberately trying to run time off the clock is to *control the game clock*. If a team is losing late in the game, they will try to 'control the game clock' by throwing the ball. That will hopefully conserve the clock because they don't have much time left to catch up. Here's the basic idea. If you're ahead and want to waste time, run the ball. If you're behind, you need to throw it. And here's what happens **"WHEN YOU NEED TO SCORE QUICKLY"**.

🐨16 WHEN YOU NEED TO SCORE QUICKLY

When you need to score quickly, it's time for the *2-minute drill*. No, not that 2-minute drill, but the goal is the same. Score in two minutes or less. When a team is trying to score with a couple of minutes to go in the first half or at the end of a game, they will go to a 2-minute drill. The team is in a 'hurry up' offense where the quarterback quickly tries to complete passes to receivers near the sideline. When a receiver catches the ball, he can run out of bounds, which stops the clock and hopefully gives the offense time to score.

There is also something called the *red zone offense*. When the offense is inside the opponent's 20-yard line, they are in the *red zone*. Once the offense is in the red zone and less than 20 yards from scoring, they are expected to get the ball in the end zone. The coach and fans aren't very happy if their team makes it all the way to the red zone but can't score. Lack of scoring on any field can be a source of frustration.

The defense also has a strategic mission and it's not just about defending their territory to prevent the other team from scoring. The defense likes to get in on the scoring action as well. These guys want a piece of the action and everyone knows that no man likes to be out-scored. Who can blame them?

The defense is doing everything they can to push the offense back to the offense's own territory. And if they push the offense all the way back to the offense's own end zone and tackle the ball carrier in that end zone, the defensive team is rewarded with 2 points. This result is called a safety. Not to be confused with the defensive back that is also called a safety. To make things more confusing, in addition to having just scored 2 points, that same team gets to receive the ball on the ensuing kickoff which provides them with a consecutive opportunity to score.

Some teams have defenses that are notorious for being able to score in another way. That's because they know how to take the ball away from the offense. Some defensive players literally strip the ball away from an offensive player's hands. When an offensive player loses possession of the ball by being stripped or dropping it, that is a *fumble*. When a ball is fumbled, both teams fight to recover it for a *fumble recovery*. When the defense recovers the fumble, their offense then comes on to the field to take over at the point where the ball is down. Sometimes the defense may recover the fumble without being tackled and return it for a touchdown. If the offense recovers the ball, they too can pick up the ball and run with it or continue possession of the ball where the fumble is ruled down.

A fumble is also considered to be a *turnover* for the offense if the defense gains possession of the ball. Another type of turnover is an *interception* where the defense intercepts or catches a pass. Any defensive player can intercept the ball, but more likely it will be a defensive back or linebacker. And you can bet anyone who intercepts or picks off a pass will do their best to try to return it for a touchdown or at least run it back as far as they can before being tackled. Nothing gets a team more fired up than when their defense scores!

The defense may like to try to score, but that usually happens when a defensive player is in the right place at the right time. Just like a successful relationship, it is usually more skill and luck than actual strategy. However, some of these basic defensive strategies are apparent. For instance, it's evident that the defense expects the offense will try to pass the ball when a linebacker or maybe a defensive back or two come up to the line of scrimmage before the play begins. The defense is going to try to rush the quarterback, which is also called *blitzing*. Watching out for the blitz is always something the offense can expect especially on

'3rd and long situations'.

When it comes to men, however, always expect the unexpected. And that goes for the coaches, too. Occasionally, a coach will go with just the opposite of the predicted play to keep you and the opponent on your toes. For example, he might fake a field goal or a punt and throw the ball instead. Maybe he will 'go for it on 4th and 1' when he doesn't really need to, just because he thinks he can. You know the type! If his team gets the 1st down in that situation, he's the man! But if they don't, he's a bum and fans will want to have his 'you know what' run out of town! Typically, with the tips you've just learned, you can also predict what will happen in basic situations. But you have to be careful, because **"FOOTBALL CAN LEAVE YOU HIGH AND DRY"**.

17 FOOTBALL CAN LEAVE YOU HIGH AND DRY

Everyone has a dry spell every now and then and sometimes it can be football related. If a guy's team loses a big game, gals can find themselves losing out as well. You know what I'm talking about here.

Now there are specific categories that men fall into after a game. There are the 'winners' who love life and the 'high and dry' thing is not an issue. If he's not a winner, he could be a 'whiner', or he might be one of those 'leave him the hell alone' guys. Hello 'high and dry'!

If guys get too emotional about a game, there might be an underlying circumstance that causes the losers to fall into these categories. If a guy is upset, even though his team is winning or he's rooting 'against' his favorite team, the red light should go off here. That's a dead give away that he probably has a bet on the game. His team may be winning the game, but by 'how much' is the question. In the gambling world, how much a team is expected to win by is called the *point spread*.

Since women gamble on men all the time, why not partake in a little friendly football wager yourself once in a while? Understanding how the point spread works may be beneficial. When you get to know the game and want to join in on 'the football pool' at work or with friends, picking the winner may be based on the point spread. In some football pools, you only have to 'pick the winner' of the game. But if you have to 'pick the spread', here's how it works.

Odds makers in Las Vegas pick the team that is favored to win and call that team the 'favorite'. The team picked to lose is the 'underdog'. They also predict by how many points the 'favorite' should beat the 'underdog', which is the 'point spread'. Many factors are taken into account when picking the favorite. One that's easy to remember is looking at which team is the visitor and which team is home. Playing at home is called *home field advantage* and is believed to be a bonus for any team because of factors such as fan support. Some teams rarely lose at home, no matter who they play. Be careful of the guys who invite you to their house!

It's pretty easy to determine who is the visitor and who is home. Unless it is noted otherwise, when you see a game listed, the visitor is always first or on top and the home team is always second or on the bottom. It's that way for every sport. Just remember when you're on the bottom, you're home.

Now that the top and bottom thing is clear, back to betting the spread. Let's say the odds makers have this game to pick; the Blue team (visitor) is playing at the Red team (home). Odds makers pick the visiting Blue team as the underdog and the home Red team as the favorite.

For betting purposes, the oddsmakers give the underdog some extra points to even the playing field. As the underdog in this example, the Blue team gets 3 and a half points. The point spread is 3 and a half, so that means the Red team, or favorite, will need to score at least 4 more points than the underdog Blue team to be the winner of the bet. Likewise, if the favorite fails to finish with at least a 4 point lead, the underdog has won the bet.

This is how an odds sheet may look. The visiting team is listed first, the point spread in the middle and the home team is last. The favorite is in capital letters.

Visitor	Points	Home
Blue	+3 1/2	RED

Here is another example with the GREEN team playing at the Black team. The GREEN team begins the game minus 6 and a half points in the hole. As a 6 and a half point favorite they will need to score at least 7 points more than the underdog Black team to win the bet. Likewise, the underdog Black team wins the bet if the favorite fails to finish with a 7 point lead or better. What ever happened to simply winning or losing?

Visitor	Points	Home
GREEN	-6 1/2	Black

Understanding the 'point spread' takes a little bit of practice, but it's a good bet that any betting man will be impressed that you know how to work the numbers! And in the event that your knowledge of the spread helps you to a little spare change of your own, you could put it to good use on **"THE ROAD TO THE SUPER BOWL PARTY"**.

18 THE ROAD TO THE SUPER BOWL PARTY

The Super Bowl Party is the big social event of the year. Even people who don't like football watch some of the game on Super Bowl Sunday, at least in between the Super Bowl commercials!

One of the major reasons that people don't watch football is because they don't know anything about it. Making an embarrassing comment about the game in front of die hard football fans can lead you straight to the kitchen or sometimes even out the front door. One woman shared this Super Bowl blunder. Her business was in technology and someone asked her who was leading in the game. Without hesitation she said Packard Bell. What she meant was the Packers, as in Green Bay Packers. Close, but certainly no cigar, and definitely no brownie points.

In order to avoid that fiasco, pick up a newspaper or go on the Internet during the football season and look at the NFL section. Memorize the teams and their nicknames. While browsing on-line, take a peak at the players without their helmets. One must avoid the fundamental error of judging a 'book' by its tight pants. And here's another thing. It's imperative to know that *NFL* stands for the *National Football League*. The league is divided up in to two conferences, the *AFC*, or the *American Football Conference* and the *NFC* or the *National Football Conference*. Each conference is also divided up in to *divisions*.

There are now 32 teams in the NFL, so get to know them all and at least know what conference and division your 'favorite' team is in. This will take some time, but it will certainly be worth it.

The road to the *Super Bowl* for all of the teams officially begins in July when teams host rigorous training camps. Then there are pre-season games and finally the regular season, which usually runs from September to early January. Each team plays a total of 16 games with one week off during a 17-week regular season. The one week that the team has off is called the *bye week*.

Teams will compete within their division and conference for the right to make the *playoffs* and hopefully a spot in the Super Bowl. Based on their winning and losing record, division champions are crowned in both the AFC and NFC. That guarantees those teams a spot in the playoffs. Teams that don't win division championships still have a chance to make the playoffs if they have a good enough record to earn a *Wild Card* spot.

The division champs and the Wild Card teams play for the conference title with the AFC Champion and the NFC Champion advancing to the Super Bowl, which is held at the end of January or early February. NFL schedules are available months before the season begins, so you'll have plenty of time to think about your party **"IN YOUR FANTASY"**.

19 IN YOUR FANTASY

It's safe to say that men and women probably don't fantasize about the same things, or do they? A man's fantasy about football has stretched into a league of its own. Fantasy football is very popular among men, but women are getting into the fantasy thing too.

Fantasy football is played by several people who form their own league. Each person owns their own team and selects real NFL players from various teams for their fantasy roster. The idea is to choose players who score a lot of points. Each week you can find fantasy football owners rooting for specific players from many different NFL teams because statistics from actual games played are used to determine points for the fantasy teams. The person with the most points at the end of the football season is the Fantasy Champion.

Fantasy football takes up a lot of time, however. It's one thing to be a football fan, but if his real 'fantasy' is football, you may want to find another man! Fantasy is not the only game in town, however. There are other leagues including NFL Europe, the Canadian Football League, the Arena League and semi-pro leagues. Women also have leagues of their own these days. And we can't forget perhaps the most fun of all, the coed flag football leagues where guys and gals play together! There is also the local 'Once a year Thanksgiving Day League' played in a neighborhood near you. This football fun seems to never end, doesn't it? That brings us to the final question, **"IS IT OVER YET"**?

20 IS IT OVER YET?

Sometimes you just have to ask yourself, is it over yet? Not anymore! Now you know enough to actually enjoy it as it's happening. No more wishing for the game to be over! Hopefully you've enjoyed this 'quickie' guide to football and smiled a bit along the way. Keep it close and use it when you need a reminder. But here's something really worth remembering. A good line might get you there, but a good heart will keep you there. Someone who's honest and plays by the rules is always a winner in my book. I know, this IS my book.

As a basic guide to pro football, and other stuff, there is much more for you to learn than what was covered here. Getting to know the game of football is like getting to know a man. It's a process and you may not understand everything but at least you're trying.

Some helpful ways to continue your relationship with football are through your relationships with men. Keep the spark alive with videos. Not those videos. Learn to play his favorite football 'video game'. While watching a game, ask him for an explanation of something that happened, but make sure the time is right and wait for a break in the action! Ask for help filling out your football pool. Guys love to think, that you think, they're smart. And the smartest thing that you can do is relax and **LEARN TO LOVE IT**!

FROM THE AUTHOR

Little did I know that childhood memories of playing touch football in the backyard with my brothers and neighborhood kids would have this kind of effect on me! Since childhood football has always been my favorite sport.

Growing up in rural Nebraska meant going to school, going to church, and playing sports. Saturdays in the fall meant Big Red Football – the University of Nebraska Cornhuskers.

It's been a fun journey from those days in Nebraska to Washington, DC. Working as a sports reporter/anchor, I covered the Washington Redskins. After teaching their Chalk Talk 101 program, I realized that I wanted to write this book, a fun and stimulating way for women to understand some basics of pro football. I hope you learn to love it as much as I do.

GLOSSARY OF FOOTBALL TERMINOLOGY

AFC: The American Football Conference - one of the two conferences in the NFL. Formed in 1970 when the American Football League merged with the National Football league.

Assistant coaches: Provide support to the Head Coach and are responsible for coaching specific player positions.

Audible: The change of the intended offensive play by the quarterback when he steps up behind the center and sees how the defense has lined up. The Q-B yells out the new play to his teammates.

Automatic 1st down: The offense earns an automatic 1st down on certain defensive penalties in addition to gaining yards.

Backfield: Players who are positioned behind the line of scrimmage.

Ball carrier: Any player running with the ball.

Blitzing: The defense rushing to get to the quarterback.

Blocking: A player using his body to keep a defender away from the player with the ball.

Boundary line: A white line several feet wide painted around the football field as a border.

Bye week: One week during the regular season when a team does not play.

Center: A player in the center of the offensive line who snaps the ball to the Q-B.

Chain gang: The guys on the sideline who keep track of marking the spot of the ball, the down and the necessary line.

Clipping: A violation by the offense or defense where a player illegally blocks an opponent below the waist from the back.

Coin toss: The flip of a coin at the beginning of the game to determine which team gets to decide whether they want to kick off or receive.

Complete pass (Pass completion): Throwing the ball forward to a player who catches it in bounds.

Control the game clock: Utilizing the time remaining in the game to either run the clock out when a team is leading or stopping the clock if a team is trailing.

Cornerbacks (Corners): A defensive back that covers the corner of the field.

Crossbar: The horizontal bar of the goal post that connects the two uprights.

Dead ball: The ball is dead when the whistle blows and the play is over.

Dead ball fouls: A violation after a play or before a play begins.

Defense: The team that does not have the ball and tries to keep the offense from scoring.

Defensive back (Defensive backfield): Defensive players in back of the defensive linemen and linebackers which include safeties and cornerbacks, also called the secondary.

Defensive coordinator: Coach responsible for calling the defensive plays.

Defensive ends: Defensive linemen on the end of the defensive line.

Defensive line (Defensive linemen): Players on defense lined up on the line of scrimmage including defensive tackles and defensive ends.

Defensive line coach: One of the specialized assistant coaching positions responsible for the defensive line.

Defensive tackles: Defensive linemen in between the defensive ends.

Delay of game: A violation by the offense when the ball isn't snapped before the play clock expires.

Divisions: The AFC and NFC are divided up in to smaller groups called divisions. Each division crowns a division champion.

Down: A team's attempt to move the ball toward the opponent's goal line. A team gets 4 downs to gain 10 yards to earn another set of downs and keep possession of the ball.

Down marker: The tall marker held by one of the members of the chain gang on the sideline to mark the spot of the ball and number of the down.

Drive: The series of plays a team runs while they are on offense.

Encroachment: A violation by any player except for the center who moves in to the neutral zone and makes physical contact with an opponent before the ball is snapped.

End lines: The shorter ends of the boundary line.

End zone: The ten yards of territory between the end line and the goal line where a touchdown is scored.

Extra point (P-A-T or Point-after-touchdown): Kicking the ball through the uprights of the goalpost to earn 1 point after a touchdown.

Facemask: A violation by any player on offense or defense grabbing the protective bars or facemask of an opposing player's helmet.

Fair catch: A player raising one arm in the air during the kick or punt to signal that he will fair catch the ball and not try to run with it. After the signal, the defense cannot touch him and the ball is marked down at the point of the catch.

False start: A violation by an offensive lineman moving from a set position before the ball is snapped.

Field goal: Kicking the ball through the uprights of the goalpost to earn 3 points.

Field goal unit: The 11 players on special teams for both offense and defense that are on the field during a field goal attempt.

Field of play: The area of the football field within the boundary line.

Field position: The position of the ball on the football field. The offense is said to have good position when near the opponent's goal line and bad field position near their own goal line.

Formation: The position of players on the field before a play begins. There are several different offensive and defensive formations.

Forward progress: The forward movement of the football.

Foul: Breaking a rule of the game punished by a penalty.

Fumble: Losing possession of the ball by being stripped or dropped.

Fumble recovery: Gaining possession of a fumbled ball by either the offense or the defense.

Goal line: The white line that is 10 yards from the end line. Crossing the goal line into the end zone will score a touchdown.

Goalpost: The tall structure in the end zone consisting of a crossbar and two uprights. Kicking a ball through the uprights will score a field goal or extra point.

Guards: Offensive linemen on each side of the center.

Going for it: A team risks running or passing the ball on 4th down instead of punting or attempting a field goal.

Hash marks: The short lines near the center of the field. The ball is always positioned in between the hash marks to begin a play.

Head Coach: The coach ultimately responsible for all decision making.

Headsets: The headgear worn by coaches to communicate with each other during the game.

Holding: A violation for the illegal use of hands or arms to grab or hold any part of an opponent's body or uniform.

Home field advantage: A team has an advantage by playing at home due to fan support, familiar surroundings and not having to trave.

Huddle: The gathering of the team on the field before each play where the quarterback tells the offense what play will be run and the snap count. A linebacker informs the defensive play to his teammates.

In bounds: The area of the field inside the boundary line.

Incomplete pass (Incompletion): A pass that is not caught or is caught out of bounds.

Interception: A player on defense catches or intercepts the ball.

Kick returner: A player who catches the ball on a kickoff and attempts to return it.

Kicker: A player who kicks the ball off a tee during a kickoff, field goal, or extra point attempt.

Kickoff: A play to start the game, the second half, overtime, and restart play after a team scores. One team kicks the ball off of a tee to the other team.

Left guard: An offensive lineman on the left side of the center.

Left tackle: An offensive lineman on the left side of the left guard or a defensive tackle on the left side of the right defensive tackle.

Line of scrimmage: The imaginary lines for each team separated by the neutral zone where a play begins.

Linebackers: Defensive players in back of the defensive line and in front of the defensive backs.

Live ball: The ball is live when the center moves the ball to snap it to the quarterback and also when it is kicked off the tee up until an official blows his whistle.

Midfield: The middle of the field, or the 50-yard line.

Necessary line: The line that a team needs to reach to earn another 1st down. Also the yellow graphic television effect that you see on TV.

Neutral zone: The area in between each team's line of scrimmage where the ball is placed.

NFC: National Football Conference - one of the two conferences in the NFL. Formed in 1970 when the American Football League merged with the National Football league.

NFL: National Football League. Formed in 1922 when the American Professional Football Association renamed itself the National Football League. Merged with the American Football League in 1970.

Offense: The team that has possession of the ball and is trying to score.

Offensive coordinator: The coach responsible for calling the offensive plays.

Offensive line (Offensive linemen): The seven offensive players lined up on the line of scrimmage including the center, guards, tackles, tight end and wide receiver.

Offensive tackles: Offensive linemen to the immediate left and right of the guards.

Official: The seven men on the field wearing striped shirts who make sure the players and coaches follow all of the rules.

Offside: A violation by any player except for the center who has any part of his body in the neutral zone before the ball is snapped.

Out of bounds: A player is out of bounds if any part of his body touches the boundary line or any area outside of the boundary line.

Overtime (O-T): The extra time in a game necessary to break a tie.

Pass interference: A violation usually committed by a defensive player or occasionally by an offensive player when illegal contact is made with an opponent during a pass play.

Penalty: The punishment handed down to a team following a violation of a rule or rules.

Penalty flag: The yellow flag an official throws to the ground when he sees a rule violation.

Play: The action by a team to try to move the ball down the field that begins with a snap and ends when an official blows his whistle.

Play clock: A clock showing the offense how much time they have before the ball must be snapped.

Playbook: A book compiled of a huge amount of plays that players must memorize.

Playoffs: Games that are played following the regular season where teams have earned the right to play off for the conference championship with the winners going to the Super Bowl. Also known as the post season.

Pocket: The area behind the line of scrimmage where a quarterback is protected by the blocking of his teammates.

Point spread: The number of points a team is predicted to win by in a game.

Point-after-touchdown (P-A-T or Extra point): Kicking the ball through the uprights of the goalpost to earn 1 point after a touchdown.

Possession: Having control of the football.

Punt: A 4th down kicking play where the punter drop kicks the snapped ball to the opposing team who tries to return it.

Punter: A player who catches a ball snapped in the air and drop kicks it to the opposing team.

Pylon: A soft orange marker at each of the four corners of the end zone that is in bounds when touched by a player or the football.

Quarterback (Q-B): The most important offensive player who runs the show and either hands off the ball or throws it to a receiver. Sometimes the Q-B may also run the ball.

Receiver: An offensive player who attempts to catch the ball.

Red zone: The twenty yards of territory between the 20-yard line and the end zone.

Red zone offense: The offensive play calling for a team that is within 20 yards of reaching their opponent's end zone. A team is likely to score when reaching the red zone.

Referee: The head official who wears a white cap while the other six officials wear black caps.

Right guard: An offensive lineman on the right side of the center.

Right tackle: An offensive lineman on the right side of the right guard or a defensive lineman on the right side of the left defensive tackle.

Roster: The list of 45 players eligible to play in a game.

Running back: An offensive player who generally runs the ball. There are different kinds of running backs including tailbacks, halfbacks, and fullbacks.

Running backs coach: One of the specialized assistant coaching positions responsible for the running backs.

Sack: A defensive player tackles the quarterback with the ball behind the line of scrimmage.

Safety: The defensive team earns 2 points for tackling the offensive team in their own end zone.

Safeties (Safety): A defensive player who covers the backfield along with the cornerbacks.

Scrambling: The quarterback running away to avoid the rush of the defense.

Secondary: Defensive players in the backfield including safeties and cornerbacks.

Set of downs: The 4 chances a team has to gain 10 yards.

Short week: Playing games with less than a week in between.

Shotgun: The position of the quarterback a few feet behind the center who has to shoot the snapped ball up in the air to the quarterback.

Sidelines: The longer sides of the boundary line.

Snap: Handing of the ball by the center between his legs to the quarterback.

Snap count: The verbal signal from the quarterback to initiate the snapping of the ball by the center.

Special teams: Players on the field during special plays including the kickoff, punts, attempting field goals and extra points.

Spiking the ball: A player throwing the ball to the ground after scoring a touchdown.

Super Bowl: The NFL's championship game between the conference winners of the AFC and NFC.

Tackle: Bringing the ball carrier to the ground.

Tackles: Offensive linemen on each side of the guards and the defensive linemen in the center of the defensive line.

Tee: The plastic stand used to place the football on during a kickoff.

Territory: A team's own area from the end line to the 50-yard line that they try to protect from the opponent.

Tight ends: An offensive player on the line of scrimmage lined up right next to one of the tackles. A tight end is also a receiver and usually a good blocker.

Time of possession: The duration of time that a team has had control of the ball.

Touchback: The placement of the football at a team's own 20-yard line following a kickoff or punt when the returner downs the ball in the end zone or the ball goes out of the end zone.

Touchdown (TD): Carrying the ball by a player or passing from one to another into the opposing team's end zone to score 6 points.

Turnover: Inadvertently turning control of the ball over to the opponent by fumbling or getting a pass intercepted.

2-minute drill: The plays called to score quickly with a couple of minutes to go in the first half or at the end of a game.

2-point conversion: Running or passing the ball in to the end zone after a touchdown for an extra 2 points.

Uprights: The two vertical poles extending upward from the crossbar of the goalpost.

Wide Receiver (Wide out): An offensive player who is a receiver and is positioned on or just behind the line of scrimmage wider out near the sideline.

Wild Card: A spot in the playoffs for teams with a good enough record that did not win a division title.

Yard lines: The lines that mark the 100 yards of playing field inside the boundary line numbering from 1 to 50.

ABOUT THE AUTHOR

Kaye Lake is an avid sports enthusiast and her cover girl looks are a counter point to her vast knowledge of sports. She developed a passion for sports early with track, basketball, volleyball, softball, football and golf.

Kaye grew up in rural Nebraska. Excelling at sports she was an All State basketball player in high school.

A graduate of the University of Nebraska-Lincoln, Kaye began her broadcasting career as a radio personality and as the public address announcer for the University of Nebraska women's basketball and volleyball teams.

As a high school coach, Kaye encouraged young women to not only participate but to also learn about sports.

Kaye is an experienced television and radio sports reporter/anchor. She reported on the NFL's Washington Redskins along with other professional and collegiate sports. In addition to sharing her love of sports as a public speaker, Kaye is also an expert in Scotch Whisky and does group tasting presentations nationally.

To book Kaye for a personal appearance or order additional copies of LEARN TO LOVE IT, log on to her website.

www.learntoloveit.net